Philip Buchan is a solicitor specialising in land law and in particular countryside matters. He qualified in 2005 (Writer to the Signet, 2016).

Philip regularly publishes articles in sector newsletters and magazines and national newspapers such as the Scotsman. He also blogs on forestry, land reform and agricultural matters.

A Practical Guide to the Law of Forests in Scotland

A Practical Guide to the Law of Forests in Scotland

Philip Buchan WS
LLB, Dip LP
Solicitor

Law Brief Publishing

Published 2021 by Law Brief Publishing, an imprint of Law Brief Publishing Ltd
30 The Parks
Minehead
Somerset
TA24 8BT

www.lawbriefpublishing.com

Paperback: 978-1-913715-28-1

Dedicated to Elspeth, Jamie, Rafe and Rose

PREFACE

In this practical guide I have aimed to provide a concise, accessible introduction to the specialised subject of forestry law.

There are no footnote references or tables of statutory materials or cases but I have tried to provide references to key sources of information throughout.

I have avoided 'legalese' and technical terminology and where unavoidable I have supplied an explanation in the hope that the book will be a useful tool for anyone with an interest in Scotland's forests whether large commercial plantations or small woodlands.

I would like to thank my publishers for their encouragement and guidance through to publication.

I would like to thank Tim Barratt, Tom Black, Sam Booth and Jock Galbraith for talking to me when I had the idea for this book. I am also very grateful to Christine Scott for editing my draft manuscript.

Finally, I thank my wife, Elspeth, for her love and support while I wrote during lockdown.

I have tried to state the law as I saw it as at 1 February 2021.

Philip Buchan
February 2021

CONTENTS

CHAPTER ONE

FORESTRY LAW HISTORY AND LEGISLATION

World War I

The importance of effective forestry management became evident in the early 20th Century. There was no clear forestry strategy in the UK prior to World War I and by the end of the War there was a critical shortage of timber and an over-reliance on timber imports. Prime Minister David Lloyd George commented that Britain came nearer to losing the war through lack of timber than want of food.

Woodlands and Forests

The UK Forestry Standard describes a forest to be land for the most part covered in trees, whether in large tracts (generally, called 'forests') or smaller areas known by a range of terms such as woods, copses, spinneys or shelterbelts. The term 'woodland' is synonymous with forest in the Standard.

The Acland Committee

In 1916, the Government appointed a committee, chaired by Francis Acland, to examine 'the best means of conserving and developing the woodland and forestry resources of the United Kingdom, having regard to the experience gained during the war'. The Acland Report was published in 1918 and recommended the creation of a 'Forest Authority equipped with funds and powers to survey, purchase, lease and plant land and generally to administer the areas acquired with compulsory powers to be exercised when needed after due enquiry and the award of fair compensation'.

Forestry Commission

The Government set up an interim Forest Authority in 1918 and the Acland Report led to a Forestry Bill. The Forestry Act 1919 came into force on 1 September of that year and established the Forestry Commission to administer woodlands in England, Scotland, Wales and Ireland.

World War II

The Forestry Commission was restructured at the beginning of World War II so that the Forest Management Department would carry out the Commission's usual activities and the Timber Supply Department would focus on wartime timber demands. By the end of WWII, approximately one-third of the UK's available timber had been felled and processed by the Women's Timber Core (known as the "Lumberjills") and thousands of overseas workers who managed the timber during the war effort.

Sustainable Forest Management

During the 1980's, global concerns about environmental degradation and deforestation focused attention on the sustainable management of forests which was first articulated at the 1992 United Nations Conference on Environment and Development (the 'Earth Summit') in Rio de Janeiro.

Forestry Legislation

The Forestry Act 1919 gave the Forestry Commission wide powers to acquire and plant land, promote timber supply and forest industries, undertake education and research, make grants and give advice to woodland owners.

The Forestry Act 1967 consolidated the Forestry Acts 1919 to 1963. The Forestry Act 1967, as amended, remains the key statute relating to forestry in England and Wales while the Forestry Act (Northern Ireland) 2010 governs forestry policy in Northern Ireland. The 1967 Act provided the regulatory basis for forestry in Scotland until it was replaced by new Scottish legislation.

The Forestry and Land Management (Scotland) Act 2018 is the first forestry legislation since the new Scottish Parliament was formed in 1999. The Forestry and Land Management (Scotland) Act 2018 (Commencement, Transitional and Saving Provisions) Regulations 2019 brought the 2018 Act into force on 1 April 2019 and the Act resulted in the devolution of forestry regulation to the Scottish Government and requires the Scottish Ministers (the group of senior Ministers in the Scottish Government) to promote 'sustainable forest management' and to publish a 'forestry strategy' (Chapter Two) setting out a vision for forestry in Scotland.

In preparing or revising the forestry strategy, the Scottish Ministers are required to have regard to:

- the land use strategy (prepared under section 57 of the Climate Change (Scotland) Act 2009
- the land rights and responsibilities statement (section 1 of the Land Reform (Scotland) Act 2016)
- Article 2 of the Kyoto Protocol to the United Nations Framework Convention on Climate Change)
- the code of practice on deer management (section 5A of the Deer (Scotland) Act 1996)
- the Scottish Biodiversity Strategy (prepared under section 2 of the Nature Conservation (Scotland) Act 2004)

The main legislation impacting on Scottish forestry includes:

- Acquisition of Land (Authorisation Procedure) (Scotland) Act 1947
- Occupiers Liability (Scotland) Act 1960
- Plant Varieties and Seeds Act 1964
- Plant Health Act 1967
- Countryside (Scotland) Act 1967
- Countryside Act 1968
- Control of Pollution Act 1974
- Ancient Monuments and Archaeological Areas Act 1979
- Land Registration (Scotland) Act 1979

- Wildlife and Countryside Act 1981
- Roads (Scotland) Act 1984
- Inheritance Tax Act 1984
- Capital Allowances Act 1990
- Environmental Protection Act 1990
- Natural Heritage (Scotland) Act 1991
- Taxation of Chargeable Gains Act 1992
- Value Added Tax Act 1994
- Environment Act 1995
- Deer (Scotland) Act 1996
- Town and Country Planning (Scotland) Act 1997
- Scotland Act 1998
- Abolition of Feudal Tenure etc. (Scotland) Act 2000
- Capital Allowances Act 2001
- Agricultural Holdings (Scotland) Act 2003
- Land Reform (Scotland) Act 2003
- Nature Conservation (Scotland) Act 2004
- Water Environment (Controlled Activities) (Scotland) Regulations 2005
- Income Tax (Trading and Other Income) Act 2005
- Flood Risk Management (Scotland) Act 2009
- Climate Change (Scotland) Act 2009
- The Public Services Reform (Scotland) Act 2010
- Wildlife and Natural Environment (Scotland) Act 2011
- Water Environment (Controlled Activities) (Scotland) Regulations 2011
- Land Registration (Scotland) Act 2012
- The Wildlife and Countryside Act 1981 (Exceptions to Section 14) (Scotland) Order 2012
- The Wildlife and Countryside Act 1981 (Exceptions to Section 14) (Scotland) Amendment Order 2012
- The Historic Environment (Scotland) Act 2014
- Community Empowerment (Scotland) Act 2015
- Land Reform (Scotland) Act 2016

- Community Right to Buy (Abandoned, Neglected or Detrimental Land (Eligible Land, Regulators and Restrictions or Transfers and Dealings) (Scotland) Regulations 2018
- The Scotland Act 1998 (Specification of Functions and Transfer of Property etc.) Order 2019
- The Forestry and Land Management (Scotland) Act 2018
- The Forestry and Land Management (Scotland) Act 2018 (Commencement, Transitional and Saving Provisions) Regulations 2019
- The Forestry and Land Management (Scotland) Act 2018 (Consequential Provisions and Modifications) Order 2019
- The Forestry (Exemptions) (Scotland) Regulations 2019
- The Felling (Scotland) Regulations 2019

This list is not exhaustive and the common law of Scotland may also apply.

CHAPTER TWO

SCOTLAND'S FORESTRY STRATEGY AND GOVERNANCE STRUCTURE

Governance Structure of Scottish Forestry

The devolution of forestry to Scotland was completed on commencement of the Forestry and Land Management (Scotland) Act 2018 (the 2018 Act) on 1 April 2019. Section 74 of the 2018 Act provided for the establishment of "a single agency or two agencies" to implement the Scottish Ministers' forestry and land management responsibilities. These executive agencies, which replaced Forestry Commission Scotland (FCS) and Forest Enterprise Scotland (FES), are Scottish Forestry (SF), which is responsible for policy, regulatory support and grant-conferring functions, and Forestry and Land Scotland (FLS), which is responsible for managing the Country's land known as the National Forest Estate (Chapter Three).

The governance of Scottish Forestry (SF) and Forestry and Land Scotland (FLS) will follow established arrangements for Scottish Government agencies. Each agency has had a framework document, (the 'Scottish Forestry Framework Document' and the 'Forestry and Land Scotland Framework Document'), approved by the Scottish Ministers, which define key roles and responsibilities between the agency and the Scottish Government. The SG will be responsible for the overall framework within which FLS and SF will operate. The Chief Executive of each agency will be directly accountable to the Scottish Ministers for delivering the agency's strategic policy aims and objectives.

Section 75 of the 2018 Act provides that the Scottish Ministers must provide a report on the operation of the administrative arrangements by 31 March 2024.

The Chief Forester

In terms of section 73 of the 2018 Act, a Chief Forester has been appointed by the Scottish Ministers to assist and advise them in carrying out their duties. The initial focus for the Chief Forester is as the Scottish Government's 'Head of Profession' with the aim of maintaining and promoting professional forestry standards within Scottish Forestry (SF) and Forestry and Land Scotland (FLS) and exploring opportunities for skills development and growth in the sector. The Chief Forester will work with bodies such as the Institute of Chartered Foresters.

Sustainable Forest Management

The Scottish Ministers must promote 'sustainable forest management'.

Sustainable Forest Management is not defined in the 2018 Act. However, at the Second Ministerial Conference on the Protection of Forests in Europe in 1993, sustainable forest management was defined as: "the stewardship and use of forest lands that maintains biodiversity, productivity, regeneration, capacity, vitality and potential to fulfil now and in the future relevant ecological, economic and social functions at local, national and global levels and that does not cause damage to other ecosystems."

The Forestry Strategy

The Scottish Government's Forestry Strategy 2019-2029 was introduced by the 2018 Act and envisions that by 2070 Scotland will have more forests and woodlands than at any time over the past 100 years. 18.5% of Scottish land is currently covered by forests and the Strategy aims to increase forest and woodland cover to 21% by 2032.

Both the 2018 Act and the Forestry Strategy have the principles of sustainable forest management at their core including adherence to the principle of 'the right tree in the right place, for the right purpose'. Objectives include increasing the contribution of forests to Scotland's economic growth, improving the resilience of forestry and increasing the use of Scotland's forest resources for health and life chances. The amount of native woodland in good condition should be increased as well as increasing the use of Scottish wood products in construction. Scotland has the highest forest woodland coverage of all of the UK nations at 18.5%; however, this is low in comparison to its European neighbours. The European Union average forest and woodland coverage is 38%.

The 2018 Act provides that the forestry strategy must present a vision for forestry in Scotland and must detail the Scottish Ministers' objectives, priorities and policies with respect to the promotion of sustainable forest management.

The forestry strategy is to include, amongst other things, the Scottish Ministers' objectives, priorities and policies with respect to:

- the creation of woodland
- the economic development of forestry
- targets for the planting of trees
- the conservation and enhancement of the environment by means of sustainable forest management
- the realisation of the social benefits of forestry
- the production and supply of timber and other forest products.

The Scottish Ministers must keep the forestry strategy under review and may, if they consider it appropriate to do so, revise the strategy.

Section 3 (5) requires the Scottish Ministers to revise the forestry strategy at least every 9 years.

The Scottish Ministers must publish the forestry strategy and each revision of it.

The forestry strategy was published in February 2019 and its 50-year vision for forestry in Scotland is as follows:

'In 2070, Scotland will have more forests and woodlands, sustainably managed and better integrated with other land uses. These will provide a more resilient, adaptable resource, with greater natural capital value, that supports a strong economy, a thriving environment and healthy and flourishing communities.'

The Implementation Plan

The Implementation Plan is designed to provide a baseline for delivering the Forestry Strategy, albeit with some changes as a result of Covid-19. Priority will be given to delivering support to the forestry sector and its recovery. The two-year plan will be kept under review.

Forestry contributes £1 billion per annum and 25,000 jobs to Scotland's economy through wood production, tourism and recreation. These economic activities are to be supported as part of the larger economy as we adapt to living with Covid-19.

CHAPTER THREE

MANAGEMENT OF LAND BY THE SCOTTISH MINISTERS

Under section 11 of the 2018 Act, the Scottish Ministers must manage forested land in a way that promotes 'sustainable forest management' (Chapter Two). 'Forested land' is defined in the 2018 Act and means land in the National Forest Estate that is forested (which includes land undergoing afforestation) and other forested land that is owned by the Scottish Ministers or managed by the Scottish Ministers on behalf of a third party. Forestry and Land Scotland (FLS) will manage the National Forest Estate on behalf of the Scottish Ministers.

The National Forest Estate

The National Forest Estate covers approximately 640,000 hectares or 9% of Scotland's land mass. The estate is two-thirds forested and one-third open habitat and agricultural land. Since the Forestry Commission was established in 1919, the National Forest Estate has evolved to provide a wide range of economic, social and environmental benefits to the populace and it is key to a range of Scottish Government priorities such as Scotland Performs, the Land Use Strategy, climate change commitments, the Scottish Biodiversity Strategy and the Scottish Forestry Strategy. The National Forest Estate is one of Scotland's greatest assets, developed by the many who have worked on it over the years.

The Forestry and Land Scotland Framework Document

The Forestry and Land Scotland Framework Document sets out the key roles and responsibilities between the agency and the Scottish Government. The framework document provides:-

"Plans will normally cover a period of three years. The Corporate Plan will set out Forestry and Land Scotland's outcomes and targets; high level performance indicators; and give an overview of how it will deliver these over the Plan period in line with the Scottish Government's Purpose and National Outcomes set out in the National Performance Framework."

The Forestry and Land Scotland Corporate Plan

The Corporate Plan presents a vision for Forestry and Land Scotland (FLS) as "Forests and land that Scotland can be proud of" and a mission statement "To look after Scotland's forests and land, for the benefit of all, now and for the future."

The outcomes are:

- FLS supports a sustainable rural economy by managing the national forests and land in a way that encourages sustainable business growth, development opportunities, jobs and investment
- Scotland's national forests and land are looked after; biodiversity is protected and enhanced; and more environmental services are provided to people
- everyone can visit and enjoy Scotland's national forests and land to connect with nature, have fun, benefit their health and wellbeing and have the opportunity to engage in FLS's community decision making
- FLS is a supportive, safe and inclusive organisation
- FLS is a high performing organisation

Section 17 of the 2018 Act provides that the Scottish Ministers may enter into arrangements for the management of land owned by others and for the provision of advice or assistance to other landowners.

In terms of section 15 of the 2018 Act, the Scottish Ministers must manage land in the National Forest Estate (whether owned or managed) that is not forested for the purpose of furthering the achievement of sustainable development.

Section 18 gives the Scottish Ministers power to acquire land by agreement if they consider it appropriate to do so. Subject to certain exceptions, section 19 provides that the Scottish Ministers may compulsorily acquire land that they require in order to promote sustainable forest management. These latter rights include (but are not limited to) power to acquire any right or interest or a servitude (a real right benefiting a piece of land that is enjoyed over neighbouring land owned by another) or other right over land. Section 20 allows the Scottish Ministers to dispose of land if they consider it appropriate to do so, having regard to the forestry strategy.

Under section 16, the Scottish Ministers must publish a map showing the areas of land they manage and section 14 imposes an obligation on the Scottish Ministers to gather and publish, by 1 May 2021, in a manner that they consider appropriate, information on forest holdings managed by third parties.

CHAPTER FOUR

TREE SPECIES AND HEALTH

Tree Species

Approximately three-quarters of Scotland's wooded area is made up of conifers (softwoods, with needle-like leaves) with the remainder being broadleaved species (hardwoods, with wide, flat leaves).

Softwoods come from conifers such as Sitka Spruce and Scots Pine and they account for the majority of Scottish wood production. These species are suited to commercial forestry because they are fast- growing, fast-maturing and they produce long, straight trunks which can be efficiently processed for timber.

Slower-growing broadleaved species are less suitable for timber production, in part due to timber processing challenges. However, broadleaved timber creation has increased and the biodiversity and environmental benefits of broadleaves are increasingly recognised – individual woodlands are often made up of a mixture of conifers and broadleaves. Sitka Spruce is the most common tree species used in commercial forestry but the species is native to North America rather than Scotland. The tree was favoured by foresters working on the National Forest Estate in the early years because it suited our soils and climate and the progression of landscape design has acted to soften some of the straight-edged early plantings seen on hillsides.

Transfer of Scottish Tree Health and Silvicultural Material Testing Functions

Global trade and imports of plants and timber create pathways for pests and diseases to enter the country and protecting forests means working to guard against these threats.

The principal plant health regulations are European Union regulations, amended and retained after the EU exit; however, sections 9 and 10 of the 2018 Act make the Scottish Ministers responsible for the testing of silvicultural propagating and planting material under the Plant Varieties and Seeds Act 1964 and tree health under the Plant Health Act 1967, which gives the Scottish Ministers powers to make orders to prevent the introduction and spread of forestry pests and diseases.

Scottish Forestry manages tree health in Scotland through research, surveillance of Scotland's forests and woodlands and engaging with importers, exporters, forest managers and the public. The agency can issue Statutory Plant Health Notices to make woodland owners act to contain or slow outbreaks of pests and/or diseases.

Following the initial Covid-19 pandemic lockdown, Scottish Forestry has restarted aerial tree inspections and ground surveys for *Phytophthora ramorum*, a tree disease which kills larch. The disease can be spread by those entering forests and woodlands and the advice to the public is to "Keep it Clean" and ensure that everyone cleans shoes, bikes, prams, any toys or equipment and also dogs before a forest visit. This will make a difference by preventing the spread of the disease. Information sheets and posters for the public and forest managers are available on Scottish Forestry's website as is TreeAlert, the agency's tool for reporting signs of tree pests and diseases.

Tree Health and Transfer of Ownership

Potential purchasers should obtain a valuation of the forest or woodland which should cover aspects such as tree health, access, condition of boundary features, water supply and drainage, designations (statutory protections for wildlife, landscape and cultural aspects of the countryside) and can include an investment appraisal. A potential purchaser will expect details of any timber treatment carried out by a seller to be disclosed to him prior to the change of ownership and he will want to know that, at least as far as the seller is aware, there are no known infestations or disease affecting the timber in the forest or woodland or adjacent land when ownership changes. If any such infestation or disease becomes known before ownership changes, the purchaser will want to know that he can resile (withdraw) from the missives (the contract for sale or purchase) without penalty due to or by either party.

Tree Health and Climate Change

It is thought that the greatest threat to forests and woodlands from climate change is likely to come from an increase in the frequency and severity of dry conditions affecting drought-sensitive trees. This will mean the suitability of tree species for certain regions will have to be reassessed. Climate change may also impact on the severity of current pests and diseases and lead to the introduction of new problem organisms.

The Climate Change (Scotland) Act 2009 created the statutory framework for greenhouse gas emissions reductions in Scotland and introduced targets to reduce carbon emissions in Scotland by at least 80% by 2050 with an interim target reduction of 42%.

Native and Non-native Species

Native tree species are trees that are believed to have established themselves naturally in Scotland and include alder, ash, aspen, birch, cherry, elder, hazel, juniper, oak, pine and willow. Generally, non-native species are species that have been introduced by humans to a location outwith their native range (the locality to which the species is indigenous rather than any locality to which the species has been imported), whether intentionally or not.

In terms of the Wildlife and Countryside Act 1981, as amended by the Wildlife and Natural Environment (Scotland) Act 2012, it is an offence to plant or otherwise cause to grow any plant in the wild outwith its native range, unless the planting of a non-native plant in the wild is authorised by an order made by the Scottish Ministers or under a licence issued by the appropriate authority.

The non-native tree species which are commonly used in Scottish forestry, such as Sitka Spruce, are to be found on the exempt list, specified in the Wildlife and Countryside Act 1981 (Exceptions to section 14) (Scotland) Order 2012, because their invasive impact is understood and they are deemed to be in the Country's economic interests. However, these non-native trees must still be managed in line with the UK Forestry Standard (Chapter Five).

Code of Practice on Non-Native Species

The Scottish Ministers' Code of Practice on Non-Native Species defines terms and sets out guidance and best practice for those who own, care for and manage non-native species so as not to cause harm to the environment. The Code also sets out responsibilities for relevant authorities. The four invasive, non-native plants which cause the most damage in Scotland are rhododendron, Japanese knotweed, giant hogweed and Himalayan balsam. Generally, an invasive species is any animal or plant that has the potential to spread and cause harm to the environment, the economy or health and well-being.

The Code is not law and failure to comply is not an offence; however, the court may take compliance into account if criminal proceedings are raised.

Any proposal to plant a non-exempt, non-native plant in the wild requires a Non-Native Species licence from NatureScot. Certain proposals may also require permissions from other agencies such as the Scottish Environment Protection Agency (SEPA).

CHAPTER FIVE

FORESTRY STANDARDS

The UK Forestry Standard (UKFS)

The UK Forestry Standard was first published in 1998 and has been developed by the forestry authorities in England, Scotland, Wales and Northern Ireland to set out the approach of the governments in the UK to sustainable forest management (Chapter Two).

The Standard defines a forest as: "Land predominantly covered in trees (defined as land under stands of trees with a canopy cover of at least 20%), whether in large tracts (generally, called 'forests') or smaller areas known by a variety of terms (including woods, copses, spinneys or shelterbelts)". 'Forestry' is defined in the Standard as, "The science and art of planting, managing and caring for forests". The term 'woodland' is synonymous with forest in the Standard. With limited exceptions, such as the management of individual trees (arboriculture), orchards and the management of Christmas trees, the Standard applies to all forests and woodlands in the UK.

The Standard sets out legal and good forestry practice requirements and supporting guidelines which forest managers in the UK must meet.

The requirements are in the form of categories of sustainable forest management covering general forestry practice, biodiversity, climate change, historic environment, landscape, people, soil and water.

The guidelines provide more detailed information for forest and woodland owners, managers and practitioners on how to comply with the requirements. Compliance with the UK Forestry Standard is the basis for assessing applications for felling permissions and forest plans and the awarding of grant funding for woodland creation and forest management.

The Forestry Standard is reviewed every 5 years with the input of the forestry sector and environmental stake holders and the Standard forms the basis of good forestry practice for the independent UK Woodland Assurance Standard (UKWAS).

The UK Woodland Assurance Standard (UKWAS)

The UK Woodland Assurance Standard (UKWAS) is an independent certification standard based on the requirements of international forest certification schemes (the Forest Stewardship Council (FSC) and the Programme for the Endorsement of Forest Certification (PEFC)) which confirms compliance with the requirements of the UKWAS Standard.

Timber and wood products certified by the UK Woodland Assurance Standard feature labels to give assurances about their integrity and are in much demand from individuals and organisations in the UK and beyond who wish to be sure that the goods they buy and use are from sustainable sources. In 2018, 58% of Scotland's forests were UKWAS certified.

CHAPTER SIX

FELLING

Part 4 of the 2018 Act sets out the legal framework for felling. "Felling" includes its ordinary meaning and intentionally killing a tree. Felling is regulated by the issuing of Felling Permissions (formerly known as Felling Licences) by Scottish Forestry.

Unauthorised Felling

Under Section 23, a person commits an offence if the person fells a tree unless (a) the felling is exempt because the Scottish Ministers have made regulations permitting the felling, or (b) the felling is carried out in accordance with (i) a felling permission, (ii) a felling direction, (iii) a restocking direction, (iv) a registered notice to comply, (v) a remedial notice, or (vi) a registered remedial notice.

The Felling (Scotland) Regulations 2019 add detail concerning information which must be included in an application for felling permission, restocking notices, felling directions, remedial notices, appeals against relevant decisions and compensation for refusal of felling permission and in respect of temporary stop notices.

Exemptions that do not require a Felling Permission

The Forestry (Exemptions) (Scotland) Regulations 2019 set out the exemptions to the offence of unauthorised felling.

The exempt types of felling are:-

(a) the felling, by a relevant person (which means the owner of the land on which the tree is situated or the occupier of such land who is carrying out the felling with the written permission of the owner) of a tree with a diameter not exceeding 10 centimetres measured over the bark at a point 1.3 metres from the base;

(b) the felling, by a relevant person, of a tree situated in-
  - (i) an orchard
  - (ii) a garden
  - (iii) a churchyard (which means an enclosed piece of ground in which a church stands)
  - (iv) a burial ground, or
  - (v) a public open space (which means an area which is designed and maintained for use by the public and includes, but is not limited to, a park, a public garden, an area of grass maintained for sport or recreation, or a footway or footpath but does not include any stands of trees which have a canopy cover of more than 20% within an area of 0.1 hectare or greater);

(c) subject to certain qualifications and exemptions, the felling, by a relevant person, of trees where the aggregate cubic content of the trees does not exceed 5 cubic metres in any quarter;

(d) the felling of a tree where necessary for the prevention of immediate danger to persons or to property;

(e) the felling of a tree where immediately required for the purpose of carrying out development authorised by planning permission granted or deemed to be granted under the Town and Country Planning (Scotland) Act 1997;

(f) the felling of a tree which may obstruct the approach of aircraft to, or the departure of aircraft from, any aerodrome, or which may hinder the safe and efficient use of air navigational or aircraft landing equipment;

(g) the felling of a tree by, or at the request of, an electricity operator, where-
  - (i) the tree is in close proximity to an electric line or electrical plant which is, is being, or is to be, installed by the operator, and

(ii) the presence of the tree has the effect mentioned in paragraph 9(1)(a) or (b) of schedule 4 of the Electricity Act 1989;

(h) the felling of a tree by, or at the request of, a statutory undertaker (generally, organisations with legal rights to carry out functions of a public character such as the provision of utilities), on land occupied by the statutory undertaker which would otherwise obstruct the construction of any works required for the undertaker's purposes or which is interfering with the maintenance of any works vested in that undertaker;

(i) the felling of a tree by or at the request of-

(i) Scottish Water, where the tree is interfering, or may interfere, with the exercise of any functions of Scottish Water, or

(ii) a Local Authority, where done in accordance with the Local Authority's functions under section 56(1) and (2) (a) to (d) of the Flood Risk Management (Scotland) Act 2009;

(j) the felling of a tree of the genus Ulmus (commonly known as Elm) which is affected by disease caused by the fungus Ceratocystis ulmi (commonly known as Dutch Elm disease) to such an extent that the greater part of the crown of the tree is dead;

(k) the felling of a tree on land which is subject to an agreement entered into with the Forestry Commissioners under section 5(1) of the 1967 Act (forestry dedication agreements) and which is being managed in accordance with a plan of operations approved by the Forestry Commissioners or the Scottish Ministers ("the plan"), where-

(i) the agreement is a forestry dedication agreement registered in the General Register of Sasines or the Land Register of Scotland,

(ii) any obligations in the forestry dedication agreement stated to be binding on the owner of the land are, at the

time of felling, binding on the person who is then the owner of the land, and

(iii) the felling is in accordance with the plan;

(l) the felling of a tree on land which is subject to an agreement entered into with the Forestry Commissioners under section 4(1) of the 1967 Act (forestry dedication agreements etc.) and which is being managed in accordance with a plan of operation approved by the Forestry Commissioners or the Scottish Ministers ("the plan") where-

(i) the agreement is a forestry dedication agreement which is not registered in the General Register of Sasines or the Land Register of Scotland;

(ii) the land is, at the time of the felling, owned by the person or persons who entered into the agreement with the Forestry Commissioners or by the survivor or survivors of such person or persons, and

(iii) the felling is in accordance with the plan;

(m) the felling of dead trees;

(n) the felling of a tree where required by order of a court or tribunal or by any enactment (passed legislation);

(o) the felling of a tree to which a tree preservation order related where the felling-

(i) occurs after 1 April 2019, and

(ii) is carried out in accordance with the consent of the authority which made the order or the Scottish Ministers, as the case may be, following a referral under section 15(1)(b) or 15(2)(a) of the 1967 Act;

(p) the felling of a tree that is covered by a tree preservation order where the felling is carried out in accordance with the consent of the planning authority following a referral to the authority under section 33(1)(b) of the Act.

Applying for Felling Permission, Conditions and Appeals

Scottish Forestry have produced a quick reference guide 'Tree Felling in Scotland – Getting Permission' and a comprehensive guidance document 'Felling Permission – Application Guidance'. The latter explains how to apply for a felling permission, how applications are assessed, changes to felling permissions, enforcement, appeals and compensation and also sets out some explanations of the exemptions and a summary of the unauthorised felling procedures.

Scottish Forestry recommend using their Land Information Search (LIS) online tool (which is available on their website) to help gather information about the land which may need to be considered as part of an application and they advise that you must have received consent from any necessary bodies before submitting the application, for example felling may require consent from NatureScot (formerly Scottish Natural Heritage) if the land is within a designated site.

You can apply for felling permission by submitting a standalone application. If you wish to carry out significant felling works you can submit a Long Term Forest Plan, or, where you only intend to carry out thinning works, you can prepare and submit a management plan. The application must specify whether the proposed felling involves:

- thinning (which means the removal of selected live trees to improve the growth of the remaining trees or for the sustainable management of the woodland)
- clear felling (which means felling most or all of the trees in the felling area)
- selective felling (which means the selected removal of groups of trees, identified in the application for felling permission, in the felling area)
- coppicing (the ordinary meaning of which is to cut back to ground level periodically to stimulate growth)
- the felling of individual trees

The application will be considered by Scottish Forestry's conservancy staff for the relevant area. There are five conservancies: Highlands and

Islands, Grampian, Central Scotland, Perth & Argyll, South Scotland and a national office in Edinburgh.

Under section 27 of the 2018 Act, in making a decision regarding the application, the Scottish Ministers (and thereby Scottish Forestry) must have regard to their duty to promote sustainable forest management (Chapter Two) which they do by encouraging good forestry practice in line with the UK Forestry Standard (Chapter Five).

Permissions for clear felling, selective fell or to fell individual trees are normally issued subject to standard conditions to restock (replant) the felled area within a certain timeframe and to maintain the trees until they are well established. Additional (as distinct from 'standard') conditions may also be imposed.

Scottish Forestry may only impose conditions on a felling permission which relate to (a) avoidance or mitigation of impact on communities or individuals, (b) avoidance or mitigation of impact on the environment, biodiversity or species, and (c) the retention of, or increase in, woodland cover.

Felling permissions may be varied, suspended or revoked. In addition, if an application is refused or a holder of a felling permission is not satisfied with the conditions attached to the permission, there is an appeals process. If an application for a felling permission is refused, the 2018 Act provides that reasons must be given for the refusal. In the event of an appeal, Scottish Forestry will refer the case to be heard by a different Conservancy office and if the internal review does not uphold the appeal, the appeal request is passed to the Scottish Government Planning and Environmental Appeals Division (DPEA). If the DPEA reporters uphold the appeal, the appropriate revised permission or decision will be issued.

Compensation for Refusal of Felling Permission

Section 32 of the 2018 Act provides that, subject to certain exceptions, a person who suffers a loss as a result of the refusal of an application for felling permission is entitled to claim compensation from Scottish Forestry within 12 months of the date on which notice of the decision to refuse felling permission was sent to the applicant. However, compensation is limited to the depreciation in the value of the trees that is attributable to the deterioration in the quality of the timber in consequence of the refusal of the felling permission. The claim for compensation must include a map of the felling area, a statement showing how the claim has been calculated and any supporting evidence demonstrating that the claimed losses were suffered by the claimant as a result of the application for felling permission being refused. When considering any compensation that may be payable, Scottish Forestry must not take into account deterioration in the quality of the timber that is attributable to neglect of the trees after the felling permission was refused and ascertain the value of the trees on the basis of current market prices at the date the claim was received.

Felling Directions

Sections 34 and 35 of the 2018 Act allow Scottish Forestry, who must have regard to their duty to promote sustainable forest management (Chapter Two), to issue a Felling Direction to a landowner to compel them to fell trees if it appears that the felling is required to (a) prevent deterioration or further deterioration in the quality of timber comprised in the trees, (b) to improve the growth of other trees, or (c) to prevent or reduce harm caused by the presence of the trees, for example, roadside trees which appear to be dangerous to traffic.

Scottish Forestry may only impose conditions on Felling Directions which relate to (a) avoidance or mitigation of the impact on communities or individuals, (b) avoidance or mitigation of the impact on the environment, biodiversity and species, and (c) the retention of, or increase in, woodland cover.

Felling Directions (and any conditions imposed on them) may be varied, revoked or appealed. A Felling Direction cannot be issued in respect of trees located in the places set out in regulation 4(b) of the Forestry (Exemptions) (Scotland) Regulations 2019 which are an orchard, a garden, a churchyard, a burial ground or a public open space.

Restocking Directions

Sections 36 and 37 permit Scottish Forestry, who must have regard to their duty to promote sustainable forest management (Chapter Two), to issue a Restocking Direction to a landowner where trees have been felled without authorisation or in order to enforce compliance with a restocking condition in a felling permission. Where a restocking direction has been issued to a landowner and another person, such as a new landowner, complies with the direction, the person who complied with the restocking direction may recover any expenses reasonably incurred from the person to whom the direction was issued.

Scottish Forestry may only impose conditions on restocking directions which relate to (a) avoidance or mitigation of the impact on communities or individuals, (b) avoidance or mitigation of the impact on the environment, biodiversity and species, and (c) the retention of, or increase in, woodland cover. Restocking directions (and any conditions imposed on them) may be varied, revoked or appealed.

Notices to Comply

Section 38 of the 2018 Act allows Scottish Forestry to apply to the Registers of Scotland to register a notice to comply in relation to the specific land where (a) a continuing condition such as a restocking obligation has been imposed on a felling permission and the felling has been carried out or (b) if a felling direction or (c) a restocking direction has been issued in respect of land. The notice will state the effect of the continuing condition on felling permission, felling direction or restocking direction, the date by which it must be fulfilled and a description of the land concerned. The notice would appear in conveyancing searches and alert any prospective new landowner to the obligations. Where Scottish Forestry is satisfied that the notice has been complied with or agree with a landowner that the notice is to be discharged, section 41 provides that Scottish Forestry must apply to register a notice of discharge from compliance which has the effect of discharging the relevant registered notice to which it relates.

Remedial Notices

Under section 54 of the 2018 Act, Scottish Forestry may give a remedial notice to a person if it appears to them that the person has failed to comply with a condition on felling permission, a felling direction, a restocking direction or a registered notice to comply. A remedial notice requires the person to take certain steps or stop particular activity within any timescale set out in the notice. Scottish Forestry may apply to register a remedial notice, in the same way as a notice to comply, in the Land Register of Scotland or the General Register of Sasines. Section 59 provides that in the event that a person fails to comply with a remedial notice, Scottish Forestry may enter the land to which the notice relates and take the steps or stop the activity specified in the notice (step-in rights). Section 63 allows Scottish Forestry to recover any reasonable expenses, administrative costs and interest from the person who failed to comply with the remedial notice and each owner of the land is jointly and severally liable. Scottish Forestry may register a notice of liability for expenses with the Land Registry under section 64 which would appear as an outstanding liability in any conveyancing searches. Where the liability has been settled, section 65 provides that Scottish Forestry must apply to register a notice of discharge of liability for expenses which has the effect of discharging the notice of liability for expenses to which it relates.

Criminal Offence

Scottish Forestry will investigate any reported or discovered cases of felling without permission and details may be submitted to the Procurator Fiscal which could lead to court proceedings. Fines for unauthorised felling can be up to £5,000 per tree felled and the responsibility for ensuring that felling permission is in place applies to all individuals involved in felling, not just the landowner.

Temporary Stop Notices

Section 45 of the 2018 Act applies if Scottish Forestry have reason to believe that unauthorised felling is taking place and allows Scottish Forestry to issue a temporary stop notice if it considers that it is expedient for the felling to stop immediately. This is to allows site investigations to be carried out safely and to prevent any additional damage. The effect of the temporary stop notice is to stop the specified activity for 28 days or such shorter period as is set out in the notice. Scottish Forestry must display both the temporary stop notice and a statement about the offence of failing to comply with a temporary stop notice on the land to which the notice relates. Section 47 provides that compensation can be claimed by a person who suffers loss directly attributable to the prohibition of felling (or related activity) under the temporary stop notice if the felling is found to be lawful and the temporary stop notice is revoked.

Felling and Transfer of Ownership

Where a forest or woodland is being transferred, the potential purchaser's offer will usually be on the condition that the seller has not entered into any timber harvesting contracts which remain uncompleted and no timber on the land will be cut or removed before the change of ownership. If any trees have been felled under a felling permission or a felling licence, a potential purchaser will want to see the permission or licence and he should engage his land agent or forestry advisor to check that any conditions have been fully complied with and the permission or licence covers the felling on the ground.

Timber Harvesting Contracts

Solicitors can advise on the terms of timber harvesting contracts with input on market variables from land agents or forestry advisors.

CHAPTER SEVEN

FINANCIAL SUPPORT

Financial support is available for forestry projects in Scotland and grants will be key to delivering the objectives in Scotland's forestry strategy (Chapter Two). Section 71 of the 2018 Act gives the Scottish Ministers powers to provide financial assistance including grants, loans, guarantees and indemnities and to attach conditions.

Forestry Grant Scheme (FGS)

Grants are available from Scottish Forestry under the Scottish Government's Forestry Grant Scheme for the creation of new woodland or for woodland improvement and the sustainable management of forests. An overview of the Forestry Grant Scheme and guidance booklets for the grant options for woodland creation and existing woodland owners are on Scottish Forestry's website.

FGS Woodland Creation

Successful applicants for the woodland creation grant will receive an initial planting payment together with annual maintenance payments for up to five years to help establish healthy woodland followed by a capital grant to cover expenditure such as fencing and tree protection.

There are nine scheme options with differing requirements for composition and stocking densities. The size of the grant available for new woodland creation varies depending on the species planted and the planting location on the basis that there may be an identified priority in certain areas of the country.

Support is available for Agroforestry, a form of land management that combines livestock farming and forestry. The option provides grants to help create small scale woodlands on sheep grazing pasture. Trees are grown on farm land which can provide benefits such as shelter for livestock, improved pasture growth, new opportunities for wildlife and timber for fuel.

The 'Sheep and Trees Forestry Grant Package' is a dual woodland creation grant and infrastructure grant aimed at promoting upland hill planting and raising awareness of the opportunities woodland can bring to farmers and landowners. The grant will enable successful applicants to build access routes, allowing farm land to be used productively where there is a lack of access for planting, and subsequently manage the new farm woodland as it grows. To be eligible, an applicant must be continuing to farm a significant part of the farm and planting 10-50 hectares of productive conifer. There have been calls for the initiative to widen its parameters to include native upland trees which also provide shelter for livestock and increase biodiversity.

Woodland creation grants are specifically not available for planting in existing woodlands (including grazed woodland), growing Christmas trees, short rotation coppice or fast-growing trees planted for energy production.

FGS Existing Woodland

For existing woodland owners, the scheme supports woodland improvement and sustainable management of existing woodlands. Successful woodland improvement grant applicants can receive a woodland improvement grant plus annual maintenance payments for up to five years. There are five scheme options covering:

- planning (forest plans)
- habitats and species (improving the condition of native woodlands and restoring plantations on Ancient Woodland sites to native woodland)
- restructuring regeneration (restocking and improving diversity)
- Low Impact Silvicultural System (LISS is a form of woodland management that helps to increase species and structural diversity)
- Woodlands in and around towns (WIAT is support for the improvement of woodlands near urban settlements)

Transfer of Grant Schemes

If the land or property is to be sold, the parties' respective land agents or forestry advisors should be engaged to provide details of all schemes affecting the property and to advise on the status of the schemes and the procedure for transferring them to the new landowner. They will need to check if any obligations under the schemes still subsist. A seller will want to ensure that all responsibility for the schemes will be transferred to the purchaser and the purchaser will want to ensure that the seller will continue to manage the relevant plantations or woods in conformity with the terms of the relevant schemes up until the change of ownership. If there is a forest plan, this may also need to be transferred.

A Land Maintenance Form (LMF) should be completed and submitted to the Scottish Government Rural Payments and Inspections Directorate (SGRPID) at completion of a sale/purchase to notify the department of the change of ownership. If the forest is not registered with SGRPID, the purchaser's land agent or forestry advisor should register it following completion of the purchase.

Financial Support in the Future

The future of rural support following the UK's exit from the EU is uncertain; however, it is presumed that something similar will be available and the indications are that there will be incentives in some shape or form for woodland planting, farming productivity, carbon capture, renewables, rural tourism projects and energy efficiency.

The Strategic Timber Transport Fund (STTF)

The Strategic Timber Transport Fund (STTF) is a Scottish Forestry scheme administered by the Timber Transport Forum's Project Officer (Chapter Eight) to provide funding for projects that reduce social disruption of rural communities and environmental impact by improving the sustainable transport of timber in Scotland's rural areas. In addition, the scheme aims to improve access to difficult-to-reach forests.

The fund supports projects such as improving minor public roads, creating in-forest roads, by-pass routes and timber transport by rail or sea.

One train can carry between 500-1000 tonnes of timber, the equivalent of 25-50 lorry loads and the Timber Link Service, which was supported by the scheme and ships timber from Argyll to Ayrshire, saves an estimated 8,000 lorry journeys a year.

Successful applicants typically receive 50% of the project costs. However, projects offering significant environmental, community and social benefits (such as a switch to rail or sea) could receive more. It is anticipated that the balance will be provided by local authority or forestry sector partners.

Scottish Forestry also offer a Preparatory Project Grant to assist with the up-front cost of preparing to apply for the STTF scheme.

CHAPTER EIGHT

TIMBER TRANSPORT ACCESS

Whether it be a small woodland or a large commercial plantation, it must be legally possible to access all parts of the land and timber for the present and intended purposes. This really cannot be emphasised enough.

Access is particularly important in forestry because the range of potential uses is diverse and trees must be planted, maintained, felled and timber extracted.

The long growing cycle of trees does not sit entirely comfortably with the law of servitudes because a servitude right of access over an adjoining property can be lost through lack of use over a 20-year period.

Access for timber transport may also be considered when assessing applications for financial support (Chapter Seven).

One of the great challenges facing the forestry industry is that Scotland's rural road network was not designed for modern haulage vehicles and highway maintenance has been under-funded so there is a balance to be struck between managing timber works efficiently without impacting significantly on the condition of our roads or the safety of the country's rural communities.

Timber transport can be by rail or over water but is predominantly by road and the stretch outside the forest or woodland gate will usually be by lorry.

It is important that the public roads and any bridges providing access to the forest or woodland are not subject to any height, width, length, weight or other restrictions. When forests are being transferred, the valuation report will usually explain how access is or will be taken and the offer will normally provide that the seller will exhibit a letter from the Local Authority confirming that there are no restrictions.

The Timber Transport Forum

The Timber Transport Forum is a voluntary partnership of representatives of the forestry and timber industries, local government, national government agencies, timber hauliers and road and freight associations, bonded by a Partnering Charter. The Forum was set up in 2000 to provide a hub for sharing ideas and best practice on timber haulage issues. Its aim is to encourage efficient, reliable and sustainable timber transport through: helping timber transport groups maintain relationships between the industry, local authorities and communities; promoting responsible timber haulage; encouraging investment in infrastructure to minimise the impact of timber transport on others; and encouraging measures to minimise the carbon emissions of timber transport. The Forum's business plan can be found on its website.

The Partnering Charter

The Partnering Charter commits the forum to core values being: openness, effective communication and cooperation; mutual trust, respect and integrity; and excellence and continuous improvement. The Charter provides that the partners will work together to: provide a forum where they can discuss timber transport issues, identify problems and find sustainable ways to resolve these issues; create effective consultation procedures between the partners; promote and inform best timber transport practice; maintain and promote agreed timber transport route maps; and inform timber transport planning strategy and encourage investment in infrastructure and technology to reduce the impact of timber haulage.

The Project Officer

The Forum has two sub-groups: a technical sub-group and an executive sub-group. The executive sub-group develops and reviews the workplan for a Project Officer who is responsible for delivering the Forum's business plan and administers the Strategic Timber Transport Scheme (Chapter Seven) on behalf of Scottish Forestry.

Good Practice Guides

The Forum's technical sub-group is responsible for maintaining the 'Road Haulage of Round Timber' Code of Practice and developing other technical guidance which can also be found on the website together with a Timber Transport Toolkit and a Knowledge Base. The Forum's website is an excellent source of information for timber hauliers and timber transport managers.

The Code of Practice sets out recommendations, responsibilities, key reminders and best practice covering seven areas: transporting timber, vehicle specifications, forest roads, loading timber, unloading timber, biosecurity and improving roundwood haulage. The Code is not law and failure to comply is not an offence but it has been approved by Police Scotland and has the support of the DVLA and the court may take compliance into account if proceedings are raised.

The UK Forestry Standard (Chapter Five) provides that forestry activities and businesses should comply with relevant codes of practice and industry guidelines.

Agreed Route Maps

Agreed Route Maps can be viewed on the Forum's website. These maps are developed by the timber transport groups at Local Authority level and put roadways leading to forests in one of five categories depending on the road's likely capacity to sustain timber haulage. Agreed Routes can be used for timber haulage without restriction (other than the roads traffic laws). Consultation Routes are routes which are recognised as being key to timber extraction but do not meet the standard of Agreed Routes. Consultation with the Local Authority is required before the route can be used and it may be necessary to agree when the route can be used and weight restrictions. Severely Restricted Routes should not normally be used for timber transport in their present condition and consultation with the Local Authority is required to agree a road and traffic management regime for timber extraction. Excluded Routes are either formally restricted, or are close to being formally restricted and should not be used for timber transport in their present condition. Consultation with the Local Authority is required to explore alternatives. Lastly, In-Forest Timber Haul Roads also contribute to the Agreed Routes and these may have seasonal restrictions, for example, if the land is used for sporting purposes. There may be additional height or weight restrictions or requirements for permits that are not shown on Agreed Routes Maps so it is advisable to check with the Local Authority that the public roadways can be used for timber transport.

Forest Accesses

Planning and all other necessary consents should be obtained for accesses into forests and woodlands off public roads. The UK Forestry Standard (Chapter Five) provides that forestry activities and businesses must comply with all relevant laws and regulations. When forests are being transferred, the valuation report should highlight if there have been any alterations to the access and it should be checked if planning consent has been or should have been granted for the creation of any bellmouths (curved road entrances), stacking areas, sight lines etc. Usually, offers also provide that there are no proposals to widen existing roads or to construct new roads which would adversely affect the land or any part of it.

Ordinarily, when forestry land is being transferred, the seller's solicitor will exhibit a Property Enquiry Certificate (a Local Authority certificate) which will confirm if the land is *ex adverso* (opposite to) a public roadway. The local authorities maintain lists of publicly adopted roadways.

The primary piece of roads legislation in Scotland is the Roads (Scotland) Act 1988. Generally, a public roadway includes the verges on either side of the roadway up to the physical barrier and where there is no physical barrier, the verge is defined by functional requirements. Roads Authorities often require approximately 3 metres verge width but this varies depending on the Local Authority. Sometimes Local Authorities can provide information, or even a map, on the extent of adopted roads, verges and bellmouths but not always.

Forestry junctions have their own specifications so an access onto a public roadway may have to be improved before it can be used for forestry purposes: forest accesses are formed or drained to prevent surface water discharging onto the public road; gradients are limited; surfacing may be required and road side ditches may have to be culverted to the satisfaction of the roads authority. The owner or forest manager may need areas of land for stacking timber and loading and turning lorries or rights over adjoining land to keep clear and maintain visibility splays.

Forest roads have to carry vehicles ranging from light vans to modern haulage lorries and harvesting machinery, plus vehicles of recreational users. The UK Forestry Standard includes guidelines for the planning and design of forest roads and quarries to comply with the UKFS requirements. Forestry and Land Scotland's forest road specification can be found on its website.

A high proportion of the total energy expended in the life cycle of a forest is accounted for by the construction of forest roads and the extraction of the construction material. This has a bearing on the sustainability of the timber grown. Constructing forest roads and quarries can have a significant visual impact, therefore an Environmental Impact Assessment may be required (implemented in Scotland to comply with the European Union Environmental Impact Assessment Directive, EIAs are used on certain projects, which could include the construction of forest roads and quarries or deforestation, to protect the environment). If a forest road fails, it can have very serious consequences for safety, environmental pollution and the landscape.

A valuation report will comment on the availability of stone within the forest for construction and an offer will usually specifically include all stone, sand and gravel and provide that any reservation of minerals (minerals can be severed from the ownership of the land so a prior owner may have retained the minerals when passing on title to the forest) will not prohibit the use of the stone in the forest or woodland for road construction or maintenance.

Access Rights

Where the forest or woodland does not adjoin a public roadway, the title should include a valid and adequate right of access between the property and the public roadway.

A servitude (easement) is a real right held by one proprietor of an area of land over another area of land, for example, a servitude right of pedestrian and vehicular access. Servitude rights are enforceable by the proprietor of the land that benefits from the servitude and they bind successors in title, or in other words, they run with the land. If the title deeds contain a formal servitude right, the terms will depend on how the servitude was drafted. Servitudes rights are interpreted *contra proferentem* (against the drafter) and when it comes to exercising rights, the party who benefits from the servitude must exercise the right *civiliter* (in the least burdensome manner) so it is important that the servitude rights are wide enough to allow the desired use of the forest or woodland. Usually, potential purchasers will be looking for rights to upgrade, re-align and widen access roads at the very least. Servitudes may be contained in a wider access or timber haulage agreement which could be between multiple parties.

Timber has a long growing cycle but it is possible to lose a servitude right through lack of use over a 20-year period (negative prescription), particularly, for example, if there is more than one access route into the property and one has not been used. Sellers should prepare to explain how servitude rights of access have been exercised on the ground.

It's also possible to acquire a servitude right of access through long-use over a 20-year period (positive prescription). Sometimes these come to the attention of the land agent or forestry advisor when he inspects the property and picks up on factors indicating that a route has been used over a long period of time such as signs or different generations of gates. If it is contended that prescriptive rights of access exist, the validity and extent of the rights exercised should be considered very carefully (sellers should stand ready to provide Affidavit (sworn statement) evidence to purchasers) and the rules and guidance for making a prescriptive application to the Registers of Scotland should be checked.

Practically, the access rights should also be considered in the context of what is on the ground and a land agent or forestry advisor should advise on this. The route of the access should be checked to make sure it matches the access rights. If there is a servitude right to create a road, it should be checked that the road has been built. An access route may not be adequate if, for example, a gate lodge or other such structure or feature along the route will obstruct large vehicles.

For larger plantations, there may be an access lease which is capable of being assigned and extended. For smaller forests and woodlands (perhaps where there has been a dispute in the past) neighbours may have entered into personal contracts agreeing how and when works will be carried out. An offer should help to establish the position and in any event the seller's rights and obligations should be checked carefully.

Usually, the starting point in an offer is that maintenance of the access route or routes is shared according to user but there could be other requirements such as paying a timber haulage levy into a maintenance fund per tonne of timber extracted.

CHAPTER NINE

LAND INFORMATION SEARCH, ANCIENT MONUMENTS AND OTHER DESIGNATIONS

Scotland's historic environment is the result of evolving land use and management over thousands of years and an important part of the national culture and identity. More recently, the Country's land use saw woodland cover fall as low as 4% of the Country's landmass before policy began to drive new planting in the twentieth century. The effect of forestry and agriculture on the historic environment has long been recognised and as we move forward with the Scottish Government's Forestry Strategy (Chapter Two) to increase forest and woodland cover to 21% by 2032, there is a need to balance the economic, environmental and social benefits of forestry while protecting and preserving the country's rich historic environment for future generations.

Land Information Search (LIS)

The Land Information Search is an online tool which can be used to search for designations or features affecting an area of land on the Ordnance Survey Map. The Land Information Search was developed by Scottish Forestry, Scotland's Environment and Scottish Natural Heritage (now 'NatureScot') and can be found on the Scottish Forestry website.

The Search will disclose points of note such as Scheduled Monuments, Sites of Special Scientific Interest (SSSIs), Special Areas of Conservation, Special Protection Areas, National Nature Reserves, National Scenic Areas, National Parks, Native Woodland, grant scheme data and forest plans. There is no fee for the Search.

Application forms for matters such as Felling Permissions (Chapter Six) or grants (Chapter Seven) require applicants to provide information on any features or issues and Scottish Forestry recommends that applicants make use of the Land Information Search to help gather this data. For example, an application for a Felling Permission might disclose that there is a Scheduled Monument on the land, recognise that there is a risk of damage to the monument and propose that the applicant will work with Historic Environment Scotland to identify an exclusion zone and agree terms for working within the exclusion zone.

PastMap and Historic Environment Portal

The PastMap search and Historic Environment Portal can be found on the Historic Environment Scotland website. The PastMap search can be used to find out historical and environmental insights into land and buildings such as those found in Canmore (a catalogue of archaeological sites, buildings, industry and maritime heritage maintained by Historic Environment Scotland), while the Historic Environmental Portal is to be used for live information about designated sites and places. The portal will disclose designations such as Scheduled Monuments, Listed Buildings, Conservation Areas, gardens and designed landscapes, historic battlefields, World Heritage Sites and historic marine protected areas. There is a Designations Search User Guide in the portal.

Scotland's Environment Map

Scotland's Environment has produced an online map which gathers and provides access to helpful data sets provided by partners such as NatureScot, Forestry Scotland (including their Scottish Forestry Map Viewer) the James Hutton Institute, Marine Scotland and SEPA (Scottish Environment Protection Agency).

Land Management

Designations information will be helpful to anyone dealing with a forestry project and it will inform the planning stage and the actions needed to achieve the objective. Given the situation where there is a designation affecting the land, it would be case of engaging with the relevant body and following their procedures. If part of the land is designated as a Site of Special Scientific Interest or, following the example above, there is a Scheduled Monument located on the property this may restrict what you can do with the property or may have implications for land management.

Scheduled Monuments

Scheduling is the process that identifies, designates and provides statutory protection for monuments of national importance. It is a criminal offence to cause damage to or carry out works to a Scheduled Monument without Scheduled Monument consent.

Scheduling gives Historic Environment Scotland powers of access to work on Scheduled Monuments where it appears to them that repairs are urgently required to preserve the condition of the monument and also gives powers to inspect monuments to monitor their condition.

An owner, tenant or occupier of a Scheduled Monument can appeal either a decision to include a monument in the Schedule of Monuments or to amend an entry in the Schedule relating to a monument.

Any person interested in a Scheduled Monument, in relation to which Scheduled Monument consent has been granted for works subject to certain specified conditions, can apply to Historic Environment Scotland for the variation or discharge of the conditions.

A person who has been served with a Scheduled Monument enforcement notice (where unauthorised works have been carried out on the monument) or any other person having an interest can appeal the enforcement notice on certain specified grounds.

There are compensation procedures available where a person suffers a loss in consequence of the refusal, or the granting subject to conditions, of a Scheduled Monument consent, and also where a person suffers a loss as a result of carrying out works which are rendered abortive because further works cease to be authorised.

Transfer of Forests and Woodlands

A valuation report should provide details of designations and features affecting the land. Usually, the starting point in offer documents is that there are no designations so a Land Information Search and Historic Environment Scotland searches will be useful to a seller gathering information in the build-up to a sale or to a purchaser or lender as part of a due diligence process. If a designation is identified, further investigation is required and any documentation relating to the designation should be obtained and examined. An entry in the Schedule of Monuments is a registrable deed so it is something that should be included in the Burdens section of a title sheet for land registered property and conveyancing searches in the General Register of Sasines.

CHAPTER TEN

THIRD PARTY RIGHTS

Third party rights could include private rights held by adjoining proprietors or other parties, rights enjoyed by the public or statutory rights held by certain bodies such as those conferred with designated land functions (Chapter Nine). Third party rights may impose obligations on an owner or manager and give rise to potential liabilities so it important to understand how third-party rights affect a property for land management reasons. Certain third-party rights may prevent an owner or potential owner from using the property as planned.

Formal servitudes should be evident from the title deeds to the property and searches. Additionally, a seller will usually be asked to guarantee or confirm, to the best of his or her knowledge and belief, that there are no informal servitude rights, rights of way, wayleaves or similar rights or encumbrances affecting the property. Often, there will be some evidence of third-party usage on the ground such as a pathway or part of a drainage system, so a land agent or forestry advisor should visit the site and report.

Buyers will want to have some understanding of the likely location of pipework and cables so that the land available for planting and growing trees or development is clear and the pipework and cables can be managed; however, routes are often not shown in title deeds or the route may have been changed over the years.

If the forest land forms part of a larger holding owned by the seller and the seller will retain adjoining land, the seller may wish to create new title conditions reserving rights for service media etc. over the forest land in which case the drafting of these rights should be considered carefully to ensure that these new title conditions will not restrict the use of the forest land.

Forestry and Water

It should be established if a water source on the land is serving third parties and what the obligations in the title deeds and any contractual agreement are in relation to supply and maintenance. If a water source on the land is providing a private water supply for others, the number of properties and the implications for providing them with a potable water supply should be clearly understood. Small scale supplies can be particularly vulnerable to flow diversions caused by forestry operations.

Confor is a members' organisation that represents, supports and promotes the sustainable forestry and wood products industry. Helpful guidance for forest managers and contractors dealing with both private water supplies and managing forest operations to protect the wider water environment can be found on Confor's website as part of the Forestry & Water Scotland initiative. In order to meet the requirements of the UK Forestry Standard (Chapter Five) for sustainable forest management forest managers and contractors must comply with all laws and sector guidelines.

Offer documents will usually be on the condition that a property is not in a Nitrate Vulnerable Zone and will require the seller to exhibit a letter from the Scottish Government's Rural Payments and Inspections Division (SGRPID) confirming as much. Fertiliser is not usually required in any quantity in forestry but, where it is needed in nutrient-poor sites, there are rules which apply to the management of fertiliser within Nitrate Vulnerable Zones to prevent runoff and leaching.

Wayleaves

If there are any wayleave agreements for cables crossing the property, copies can be obtained from the relevant utility provider. A potential purchaser's offer will ordinarily include a condition that the seller will not capitalise the annual wayleave payments (grant a utility provider more permanent rights in exchange for a lump sum compensation payment), the annual wayleave payments will be apportioned between the parties at completion and the utility provider will be notified of the change of ownership. If there are cables but no wayleave agreement, it may be that an agreement should be negotiated with the relevant utility provider.

Access

It has been UK policy to promote public access to forests and woodlands since the mid-20th century.

The law of access to land in Scotland is multi-layered in that access rights can be public, such as statutory access rights and public rights of way (which can be designated as core paths), or private, such as servitude rights which are enforceable only by the proprietor of land that benefits from the servitude.

The Land Reform (Scotland) Act 2003, as amended, introduced the statutory right of responsible access, (the popular term 'right to roam' does not reflect the key element of 'responsible access'), and extended the public's rights to access Scotland's land and inland waters subject to certain exceptions and guidance set out in the Scottish Outdoor Access Code as to what is responsible conduct for access takers and land managers. Whether or not an access taker's conduct is responsible will depend on the circumstances but lawfulness, reasonableness, proper account of the interests of others and the features of the land in question are important considerations.

The access rights must be exercised in ways that are lawful and reasonable and the Access Code lists some of the behavioural statutory offences such as poaching, vandalism, not cleaning up after your dog has fouled in a public place, being responsible for a dog worrying livestock, dropping litter, polluting water, and disturbing wild birds, animals and plants.

The access rights created by the 2003 Act do not extend to crossing land or water for the purposes of taking away, for commercial purposes or for profit, anything in or on the land (for example, mushrooms or berries picked for commercial use, or gravel and stones); any harvesting of non-timber products (NTFPs) must also be carried out in a lawful manner. The access rights under the 2003 Act do not allow parking a car on a landowner's land without permission.

Landowner's and managers are presumed to be acting responsibly if their actions do not unreasonably interfere with the access rights of any person, in accordance with the Access Code. The Access Code sets out indicators of responsible behaviour in forests and woods, including those with ongoing forest operations, for both the public and land managers.

As well as being wonderful places for recreation, forests and woodlands are workplaces, and the sector is also dealing with the effects of Covid-19. Forestry works are required to maintain all forests and woodlands, large and small, and owners range from private individuals, with sometimes very limited resources, to investment funds. Timber harvesting and haulage operations have been increasing over recent years; as timber crops reach maturity, so a balance of interests is required to ensure that those who are accessing forests and woodlands for recreation and work can do so safely.

The Access Code is incorporated into both the UK Forestry Standard and the UK Woodland Assurance Standard (Chapter Five). Occupiers of land, which include landowners and managers, have a duty under the Occupiers Liability (Scotland) Act 1960 to take reasonable care for the safety of people coming onto their land.

The Scottish Rights of Way and Access Society (Scotways) maintains the National Catalogue of Rights of Way and offer documents should make it a condition that the seller will present a letter from Scotways confirming that there are no public rights of way affecting the property. Information about Core Paths, (public rights of way which have been designated as Core Paths), is not held in the National Catalogue of Rights of Way but can be found by searching the relevant Local Authority's website. Applications for registration of title should include information known to the applicant about public rights of way (and Core Paths) and the Keeper of the Registers of Scotland must enter this information in the title sheet so some of these rights may already appear as burdens.

Title Deeds

The title deeds to the property should be checked to ensure that there are no burdens imposed by third parties which would prevent the property from being used for forestry purposes. If there are, and they subsist (they are still enforceable), they may have to be varied or discharged (removed).

Materials may be required for road construction and, as discussed in Chapter Eight (Timber Transport Access), an offer document will usually make it a condition that all stone, sand and gravel on the property is included and that any reservation of minerals in the title deeds will not prohibit the use of the stone in the forest or woodland for road construction or maintenance.

Clawback Agreements

Sometimes a purchaser will be asked to enter into a clawback agreement with a seller if the seller thinks there is a possibility that the land could be developed for housing or renewable energy in the future, or there may already be a clawback agreement in place between the seller and a third party which the purchaser is being asked to assume on substantially the same basis.

Clawback agreements enable the seller to claw back some of the enhanced value of the property if the purchaser takes certain steps to develop the property such as obtaining planning permission.

The method for calculating any payment due and the timing of the payment in a clawback agreement for a renewable energy development should differ from e.g. a clawback agreement for a housing development due to the long lead-in period before any significant income is received from a renewable energy project. There should be a Standard Security (a legal charge over the property) granted by the purchaser to secure the obligations in the clawback agreement. Generally, banks require loans made by them to be secured by a first-ranking Standard Security so the clawback security should be second-ranking if the purchaser is using a bank loan to buy the property. If the purchaser is not borrowing, the terms of the clawback agreement should still allow the clawback Standard Security to be ranked behind a Standard Security granted by the purchaser if he in good faith wishes to raise finance on the security of the property to fund the purchase or otherwise. The terms of both the clawback agreement and the security should be checked carefully.

Leases

An offer document will usually make it a condition that actual vacant possession and occupation of the whole of the property will be given to the purchaser at completion, and further, no part of the property is subject to an agricultural tenancy or any other form of lease or occupancy agreement. If the property is being sold subject to an existing lease or occupancy agreement, this should be mentioned in any sales particulars for the property and a purchaser will need to understand and be satisfied with the current terms of the arrangement, in particular, the provisions for termination, so the seller should prepare to provide the necessary information.

Following abolition of feudal tenure, offer documents will ordinarily make it a condition that the whole shooting and sporting rights, including the trout fishing in all rivers, lochs and streams, are included with the land. Sporting rights can be for shooting and fishing. Salmon fishings are treated differently in law and are outwith the scope of this book. Often, the right to shoot deer in a forest will be leased to a third party, and where there is fishing of some quality, there may be an arrangement on a seasonal basis. Sometimes land will be purchased and the new owner will grant a lease of the sporting rights to the seller. Whether this is a lease or a lesser contractual arrangement will depend on various factors including the degree of occupation and control. Sporting rights may be very valuable, particularly in deer forests, in which case the cull and catch records should be checked by a valuer.

CHAPTER ELEVEN

BOUNDARIES AND MAPPING

The boundaries of a forest or woodland may be made up of a combination of different land and water features and Scotland's map-based land registration regime relies on accurate mapping before a title sheet can be produced.

If the land was acquired more than 20 years ago, it is most likely recorded in the General Register of Sasines rather than registered under the land registration regime however the land could be in the Sasine register if it was acquired more recently by a method which did not trigger land registration.

It is possible that parts of the land are registered in the Land Register and parts are in the Sasine register because events such as the grant of a lease for 20 years or more, or granting a Standard Security to secure a loan have resulted in 'patches' of the land being registered in the newer map-based register.

This is an important consideration because if the land, or part of it, is registered in the Sasine register then, depending on the availability or quality of any plan or plans with the title deeds, the property may have to be mapped. Sasine title deeds for land may have a general description ('the Lands and Estate of...') rather than a plan or reference to particular features on the ground in which case evidence of possession must be considered. If a seller is retaining land and new title conditions will be created for the benefit of adjoining land, the benefiting land may also have to be mapped.

The title deeds should be checked to ensure that the legal boundaries match the description of the property in the sales particulars (which will usually include a plan), and a land agent or forestry advisor should be engaged to visit the site and check and report on the occupied extent and the condition of the boundary features. The occupied extent may not match the legal extent in which case remedial conveyancing could be required.

Usually, the thinking behind the legal boundary will become clear after looking at the Ordnance Survey Map or discussion with someone with knowledge on the ground but there may not be a physical feature on the ground marking the legal boundary and it is not uncommon for fences on high ground to follow a practical line avoiding rock or very steep ground rather than the title line. The March Dykes Act 1669 remains available to rural landowners for the purpose of producing a boundary suitable for enclosure.

Adjoining proprietors may have entered into agreements to swap land or agree boundary lines; sometimes there can be a great many of these with the title deeds with plans of varying quality, thus it can take some time for a mapper to produce a plan that correctly reflects them and complies with the requirements of the Registers of Scotland.

Therefore, if land is to be sold, it is advisable to check the registration status of the forest or woodland and as soon as the basic extent of the subjects of sale is known, if mapping is required, prepare a draft plan and obtain a Plans Report to check that the draft plan is compliant with the Land Registry's requirements.

Plans Reports

Plans reports check for conflicts against both already-registered land titles and the features on the Ordnance Survey Map: the former because the land will go into the Land Register and must not conflict with already-registered titles and the latter because the Registers of Scotland's Cadastral Map is based on the Ordnance Survey Map. Generally, Plans Reports are obtained before a property goes into the Land Register but they can also be used to highlight conflicts between registered titles which happens occasionally.

If you are dealing with a forest or woodland that is located beside any form of development, a Plans Report could potentially highlight a number of conflicts and each conflict will have to be addressed before the plan can be used to register a purchaser's title. A seller should obtain a Plans Report and address any conflicts as part of the preparations for selling the property.

Voluntary registration of title

As an owner or manager, it is certainly worthwhile checking the registration status of a forest or woodland whether or not there is an intention to sell the property due to the following benefits of having a land registered title:

- Registration means mapping the boundaries on the Ordnance Survey Map, removing ambiguity and competition in Sasine descriptions. The law protects the rights of persons who acquire land in good faith with the result that there is a benefit in mapping and registering your boundaries before neighbouring land is registered and sold

- Registering title is an opportunity to prevent access or ransom strip (an area of land which could potentially be used by a third party to hold development to ransom) issues by addressing latent problems in Sasine title deeds. It is also an opportunity to update the title by adding or removing rights and conditions, such as removing burdens which no longer subsist or adding a valuable right which has been established outwith a formal title deed, such as a prescriptive right of access over a neighbouring property. If the forest or woodland is bounded by a public roadway (Chapter Eight – Timber Transport Access), a purchaser's land agent or forestry advisor should be asked to check that access is practicable to the forest or woodland to and from the publicly adopted roadway and there are no ransom strips between the adopted extent (the area which is maintained by the Local Authority) and the land

- Land registration can consolidate and simplify complex title data and eliminate the time and financial cost of losing paper title deeds

- Dealing with registered titles makes buying and selling and granting security over property easier, faster and therefore cheaper

- A land registered title includes a state-backed guarantee of validity as at the date of registration

Boundary Fences and Maintenance

Generally, unless the title deeds provide otherwise, a fence or wall built entirely on one side of a boundary belongs to the owner of the land on which the fence or wall is built and where a fence or wall is built exactly on the line of the boundary, each landowner owns up to the mid-point of the fence or wall with the part of the boundary feature on the other side of the boundary line being subject to reciprocal common interest rights in relation to alterations or repairs. Sometimes, title deeds will specify that the boundary between adjoining properties is, for example, the outer face of the boundary fence or wall but very often not all of the boundaries of the property are specified. If the title deeds describe the property as being "enclosed by" a feature, there is a presumption in law that the whole feature forms part of the property.

If the title deeds describe the property as being "bounded by" a feature this will tend to have the effect of excluding the feature from the property; however, there are exceptions, for example, where a property is described as being "bounded by" a roadway and the roadway has been adopted for maintenance by the Local Authority, the presumption is that the boundary will be the mid-point of the roadway. Similarly, where a property is described as being "bounded by" a non-tidal river or stream, the presumption is that the boundary will be the mid-point of the river or stream. The first step when determining the boundaries of a property is to examine the title deeds.

A landowner who has sole ownership of a boundary fence or wall is allowed to maintain or remove the boundary fence or wall as he wishes. Where the boundary fence or wall is owned by adjoining proprietors up to the mid-point, each proprietor is subject to obligations in common interest to maintain the part of the fence or wall that belongs to him and not to do anything to impair the strength and stability of the boundary feature as a whole. Where the title deeds expressly declare a fence or wall to be in common ownership, either adjoining proprietor may carry out necessary repairs but one proprietor may not alter the boundary feature without the consent of the other proprietor.

The title deeds will usually confirm the maintenance obligations and where the title deeds are silent, the common law will apply. If the fence or wall is owned by adjoining proprietors up to the mid-point, each proprietor is solely responsible for the cost of repairs to his own side of the boundary feature and where a fence or wall is endangered by the failure of one party to carry out essential acts of maintenance on his side of the boundary feature, the adjoining proprietor can require that the work be undertaken. Where the title deeds expressly declare a fence or wall to be common property, either adjoining proprietor may carry out necessary repairs and look to the other proprietor for a pro rata contribution to the cost of the necessary repairs. There are separate rules for maintenance of march (boundary fences or walls) features within the terms of the March Dykes Act 1661.

A potential purchaser's offer will usually also make it a condition that there will be no liability for the seller's share of the cost of maintaining boundary features outstanding at the date of completion. Deer fencing in particular can be expensive to maintain.

Boundary enclosures adjoining public roadways would be the sole responsibility of the landowner adjoining the roadway.

A purchaser will want to be able to erect deer and rabbit proof fencing along the boundaries to protect the trees so the title deeds should be checked to ensure that there are no restrictions which would prevent the purchaser from doing so. Third party access rights have to be considered when erecting fencing because it is illegal to obstruct public and private access routes. Fencing can also have an impact on the landscape, vegetation diversity, wildlife (for example, upland birds striking fences during flight) and archaeology.

CHAPTER TWELVE

DEER MANAGEMENT

There are four species of wild deer in Scotland which can be categorised into two species of native wild deer, red and roe deer, and two non-native species, fallow and sika deer. There are also hybrids of red and sika deer. These deer live in and around the country's forests and woodlands because they browse (feed) on young trees and woodlands also provide the deer with shelter.

Adult deer have no natural predators in Scotland with the result that their numbers must be sustainably managed by humans.

Deer overpopulation leads to public interest issues such as increases in road traffic accidents, community health problems (such as Lyme disease hosted by ticks on deer), agricultural and silvicultural crop damage, costly public subsidy payments for fencing to protect new tree planting and high methane-production levels which are damaging to the environment. Deer overpopulation also harms the deer themselves, causing many animals to die during the Winter months due to starvation and lack of woodland shelter. Scotland's wild deer are a valuable economic, social and cultural asset.

The management of wild deer involves planning, organising and controlling a number of interests such as environmental and economic considerations and deer welfare.

In Scotland, wild deer in particular are considered to be wild animals and are classified in Scots property law as *res nullius* (belonging to no-one) until such time as they are killed or captured.

Generally, deer hunting rights and sporting rights are attached to the ownership of the land. However, there is some, though very limited, case law where it may have been established that the hunting rights and the ownership of the land were held by different parties, and the Abolition of Feudal Tenure etc. (Scotland) Act 2000 allowed feudal superiors, in certain restricted circumstances, to convert sporting rights (fishing or game) into a separate 'tenement' or property right distinct from the ownership of the land by process of registering a notice prior to 28 November 2004. Forest and woodland owners can lease their deer hunting rights to another person as a sporting lease (Chapter Eleven).

The Deer (Scotland) Act 1958 codified the law in relation to deer, addressing conservation and control, close seasons, unlawful taking and killing of deer, dealing in venison and enforcement. The 1958 Act also established the Red Deer Commission with powers for conservation and control. The 1958 Act set the template for Scotland's current deer legislation under the Deer (Scotland) Act 1996, as amended, which replaced the Red Deer Commission with the Deer Commission for Scotland.

The Public Services Reform (Scotland) Act 2010 changed the deer management structure by moving away from having a standalone Commission and conferring responsibility for furthering the conservation, control and sustainable management of deer on Scottish Natural Heritage (now 'NatureScot') as part of the organisation's wider wildlife responsibilities.

The Wildlife and Natural Environment (Scotland) Act 2011 amended the 1996 Act, changing the provisions which allow certain occupiers of land to shoot deer during close seasons and the exercise of control agreements, control schemes and emergency measures to manage deer. The 2011 Act also required Scottish Natural Heritage to prepare a code of practice in relation to deer management and enabled the Scottish Ministers to establish a register of persons who are competent to shoot deer.

The aim of the Code of Practice on Deer Management is "to help everybody who owns or manages land on which wild deer occur and those who manage wild deer on someone else's land to deliver sustainable deer management" and the code can be found on the NatureScot website. The code is not law but the extent that it has been complied with could be taken into account by the Court and other bodies and the UK Forestry Standard (Chapter Five) requires that all law and sector guidelines are complied with.

On 28 June 2016, sections 78-82 of the Land Reform (Scotland) Act 2016 were brought into force, giving Scottish Natural Heritage additional powers and duties in respect of the management of deer including the power to require owners and occupiers to produce Deer Management Plans within one year of service of a notice. Scottish Natural Heritage is responsible for approving the plans and it may also amend them in consultation with the local deer management group (there are around 50 such groups, represented by the Association of Deer Management Groups).

Scottish Natural Heritage must carry out a 3-yearly review of compliance and the effectiveness of the Code of Practice on Deer Management and report its findings to the Scottish Ministers.

In 2017, the Scottish Government established the Deer Working Group to review the existing statutory and non-statutory arrangements for the management of wild deer in Scotland. The Deer Working Group's Report 'The Management of Wild Deer in Scotland' is available on the Scottish Government's website and includes a number of "recommendations for changes to ensure effective deer management that safeguards public interests and promote the sustainable management of wild deer". The Scottish Government's response to the Deer Working Group's Report is expected in Spring 2021.

CHAPTER THIRTEEN

HUTTING

Reforesting Scotland is a charitable organisation which aims to: promote a sustainable forest culture and economy in a well-forested land; develop the use of locally-produced forest goods and services; encourage social and ecological restoration in forests and in wider land use; raise awareness of the benefits of low-energy living based on woodland resources and place the Scottish forestry situation in an international context.

Support for hutting has been growing steadily since Reforesting Scotland's Thousand Huts project which was launched in June 2011. Reforesting Scotland's website is an excellent source of information and guidance in relation to planning, designing, building and regulating huts and hut sites.

Reforesting Scotland describe hutting as follows:

"Hutting is the term used for the traditional model of hut use which came to the fore in Scotland between the First and Second World Wars, whereby workers from the industrial areas of Scotland paid a little ground rent to a landowner so they could build a simple hut for the use of their family and friends. Some hut sites of this type still exist in Scotland, including the largest, Carbeth, which has 140 huts on a 90 acre site. Reforesting Scotland's Thousand Huts campaign successfully lobbied for inclusion of huts in Scottish Planning Policy in 2014, enabling a fledgling new wave of hutting in Scotland."

The glossary to the Scottish Government's Scottish Planning Policy defined a 'hut' as follows:

"A simple building used intermittently as recreational accommodation (ie. not a principal residence); having an internal floor area of no more than $30m^2$; constructed from low impact materials; generally not connected to mains water, electricity or sewerage; and built in such a way that it is removable with little or no trace at the end of its life. Huts may be built singly or in groups."

Hutting is a strong part of Norwegian culture where around one-half of the population have access to a Hytte (hut) to get away from everyday life, to live simply and to reconnect with family and with nature – some of these desires may be familiar to bothying enthusiasts in Scotland.

Woodlands help to minimise the visual impact of huts while also affording hutters some privacy to enjoy the various health and wellbeing benefits of experiencing the countryside with family and friends.

Planning permission is required for the erection of a hut or the development of a hut site and a guidance booklet, 'New hutting developments: Good practice guidance on the planning, development and management of huts and hut sites' is available on Reforesting Scotland's website for the benefit of applicants and planners. All potential hutters or developers should seek the advice of a planning consultant.

Building control consent may be required for the erection of a hut and a 'Good Practice Guide to Hut Construction' is available on Reforesting Scotland's website.

Before developing a site for hutting, the title deeds should be checked to ensure that there are no title conditions or access limitations which would prevent the land being used for this purpose.

Plots may be sold or leased and, in the case of the latter, Reforesting Scotland have produced a Voluntary Code of Conduct which helpfully sets out a framework of recommended rights and responsibilities for hutters and woodland owners.

The Code recommends provisions for inclusion in a lease such as: the use of the property; the rights and obligations applicable to both parties (including obligations imposed on the hutter to comply with woodland management operations, designations, grants, schemes and biosecurity responsibilities); rent review and how the hut itself is to be dealt with at the termination of the lease.

If plots are sold, that is perhaps more likely to be as part of a site but each plot or site will have its own legal requirements. There is some guidance on rents available on the Reforesting Scotland website as well as methods for potential hutters to make contact with the hutting community. A land agent or forestry advisor will advise a woodland owner on rents and negotiate the basis for a potential sale or a lease guided by the recommendations in the Voluntary Code of Conduct.

CHAPTER FOURTEEN

COMMUNITY WOODLANDS

A community woodland is a woodland controlled by the local populace through a community woodland group. The reasons for community interest in woodlands may include a wish to safeguard a woodland for the local community, concerns about lack of maintenance, ideas for activities such as family trails or a community woodfuel business or the desire to create a new woodland.

The concept of community-managed woodlands has developed over the past 40 years in both rural and urban areas.

Reforesting Scotland provided help and support to many of Scotland's community woodlands and in 2003 the Community Woodlands Association was established as the representative body of Scotland's community woodland groups of which there are approximately 200 in number.

The Community Woodlands Association has produced a series of information sheets which are available on its website together with helpful newsletters and e-bulletins for the community woodland sector. The information sheets include advice on setting up a community woodland group, community right to buy and employing a community forester. The website also provides fundraising information.

Community woodlands vary greatly in scale and type and the most efficient business model for the community woodland group will depend on the group's objectives.

The work of the Community Woodland Association is supported financially by Scottish Forestry who support community use, management and ownership of woodlands.

The Scottish Forestry Community Fund supports community groups and organisations that encourage people to use woods more. Eligible applicants for the fund include community groups, voluntary groups, development trusts, social enterprises and charities. The Community Fund is not available to private individuals.

Eligible activities include schemes that promote: physical activity, such as the Open Aye – Winter Woodland Photo Walks project for a group of participants from Govanhill Housing Association's Minority Ethnic Residents Group; establishing volunteer groups; developing materials that promote the health and well-being benefits offered by woodlands and certain costs associated with community asset transfer scheme applications. The funding is not suitable for financing the acquisition of land.

The Scottish Land Fund aims to support rural and urban communities to become more resilient and sustainable through the ownership and management of land and land assets. Funded by the Scottish Government and delivered in partnership with The National Lottery Community Fund and Highlands and Islands Enterprise, the Scottish Land Fund offers grants of between £10,000 and £1 million to help communities take ownership of land and buildings as well as providing practical support and assistance to applicants. A list of awards made from the Scottish Land Fund is available on the National Lottery Community Fund website.

Rights to Buy

The Community Right to Buy was first introduced by the Land Reform (Scotland) Act 2003 which allows a community body to register an interest in land thereby giving the community body a pre-emptive right to buy if the landowner, subject to certain exceptions, takes any action with a view to the transfer or sale of the land in question.

The Community Empowerment (Scotland) Act 2015, which came into force on 15 April 2016, extended the geographical scope of the Community Right to Buy to include urban areas of land. The 2015 Act also introduced a new absolute Community Right to Buy abandoned, neglected or detrimental land, which was brought into force on 27 June 2018, where the owner is not willing to sell the land. This right can only be used where the community body has tried but failed to buy the land from the landowner.

The 2015 Act also created a right for community bodies to make asset transfer requests to all local authorities, Scottish Ministers and a range of public bodies for any land or buildings they feel they could make better use of for local people. Applicants can request ownership, lease or other rights as they wish.

The Land Reform (Scotland) Act 2016 introduced a broader absolute community right to acquire land for the purposes of furthering sustainable development. A community body must demonstrate that 'sustainable development conditions' are met (together with certain other criteria). The 2016 Act defines these as being met if:

- the transfer of land is likely to further sustainable development in relation to the land
- the transfer of land is in the public interest
- the transfer of land is likely to result in significant benefit to the relevant community and is the only practicable, or the most practicable, way of achieving that significant benefit
- denial of consent to the transfer of land is likely to result in harm to the community

Like the Community Right to Buy abandoned, neglected or detrimental land, there is no requirement for a willing seller and this right can only be used where the community body has tried but failed to buy the land from the landowner.

To date, it appears that in the majority of cases where a community acquisition has proceeded, a transfer has taken place by agreement between the community and landowner rather than within the terms of the statutory procedures but this may change as a result of the more recent provisions.

CHAPTER FIFTEEN

FORESTRY TAXATION

Financial support is available for forestry projects in Scotland in the form of grants (Chapter Seven) and the UK tax regime provides the forestry sector with various tax reliefs and exemptions to incentivise new planting and forestry investment.

Inheritance Tax, Capital Gains Tax and Corporation Tax are reserved matters, under the control of the UK Government. A number of the reliefs applicable to the forestry sector are summarised below.

In particular, Agricultural Property Relief and Business Property Relief are valuable benefits and owners should review their affairs to check that the qualifying criteria are met to avoid challenge by HM Revenue & Customs.

Inheritance Tax

Agricultural Property Relief (APR)

Agricultural Property Relief can be available where woodlands are occupied with agricultural land and the occupation of the woodlands is ancillary to the agricultural land. There are an estimated 60,000 farm woodland holdings in the UK and it is thought that approximately 50,000 of these sometimes small and scattered woodlands are less than 10 hectares in size.

Ancillary uses could include shelter belts (shelter belts are areas of woodland usually planted on high or exposed land to provide shelter from the wind for livestock and crops), game coverts (game coverts are small areas of woodland or thickets providing cover for game) or short rotation coppice (short rotation coppice is the intensive cultivation of trees, planted at high density, with the timber being harvested at intervals of less than 10 years) grown to produce timber for fencing or wood fuel on the farm.

Woodlands occupied for non-agricultural purposes, such as amenity woodland or woodland used for the production of commercial timber, will not be agricultural property. However, they may qualify for Business Property Relief or Woodlands Relief. Woodlands being taken out of agriculture will not qualify for the relief.

Business Property Relief (BPR)

Commercial woodland can qualify for 100% Business Property Relief from Inheritance Tax with the result that no Inheritance Tax may be payable on the owner's death on either the land or the trees. To qualify, the woodland must be managed on a commercial basis and the business must be carried out with a view to profit and have been owned for two years. If death occurs within two years of ownership, Inheritance Tax will be payable at 40% on the value of the woodlands in excess of the Nil Rate Band. Forests and woodlands managed commercially may include, for example, commercial timber harvesting or woodlands used for commercial shooting. Business Property Relief cannot be claimed against an asset if it also qualifies for Agricultural Property Relief.

Woodlands Relief

Woodlands Relief allows beneficiaries to ask for the value of the timber (but not the land) to be excluded from an individual's estate, provided that the individual has owned the woodlands for five years. This is a deferral rather than a relief, available because trees are a slow-growing crop. Inheritance Tax will be due on the proceeds received from the eventual sale of the timber.

Heritage Relief

Certain designated forests and woodlands may be exempt from Inheritance Tax under Heritage Relief. This applies to land of outstanding scenic, historic or scientific interest. A transfer of value may qualify for the relief if the new owner undertakes to maintain the forest or woodland, preserve its character and provide reasonable access to the public.

Capital Gains Tax

The sale of standing or felled timber from a woodland managed by the occupier on a commercial basis is exempt from Capital Gains Tax; however, any gains arising from the sale of the underlying land are liable to Capital Gains Tax.

Where a commercial woodland is being sold, the value of the land on the one hand and the trees, timber and saleable underwood on the other hand, is apportioned and the portion of the sale proceeds which relates to the trees growing in the forest or woodland is ignored for the purpose of calculating the tax liability.

Apportionment of the value between land and trees is not applicable to agricultural or amenity woodland. Where a forest or woodland has both commercial and amenity usage, the value of the commercial timber and the amenity value should also be apportioned. Capital Gains Tax is payable on timber when non-commercial forests or woodlands are sold, however a chattels exemption may be available.

Further Capital Gains Tax reliefs which apply to commercial woodland include:-

Holdover Relief

Holdover Relief may be available on the gains arising from the gift of commercial forests or woodlands with the effect that Capital Gains Tax is not paid when the woodland is given away but rather when the recipient of the woodland disposes of it at a later date.

Roll-over Relief

Roll-over Relief allows businesses to defer gains arising on the sale of the land by rolling over the gains against the cost of replacement assets (such as new commercial woodland) thereby postponing the tax liability until the disposal of the new woodland.

Entrepreneur's Relief

Generally speaking, the commercial occupation of woodland is not a trade for Income Tax purposes so the sale of commercial woodland does not qualify for Entrepreneur's Relief unless the woodland forms part of a wider trading business which does qualify for Entrepreneur's Relief.

Heritage Relief

Heritage Relief may also be available as a relief from Capital Gains Tax. The UK Government introduced the Conditional Exemption Tax Incentive Scheme to preserve and protect national heritage for the benefit of the public. As mentioned above, this applies to land of outstanding scenic, historic or scientific interest and a transfer of value may qualify for the relief if the new owner undertakes to maintain the forest or woodland, preserve its character and provide reasonable access to the public.

Income Tax and Corporation Tax

Income received from the sale of timber from the ownership of commercial woodlands is exempt from both Income Tax and Corporation Tax.

The Income Tax exemption does not include income received from the sale of Christmas trees or short rotation coppice cultivation.

Where a commercial woodland, or part of it, is let in return for a rent (for example, camp sites or sporting lets), the rental income is chargeable.

Value Added Tax (VAT)

It may be possible for forest or woodland owners who are registered for VAT to recover input VAT on qualifying goods and services relating to their project.

Land & Buildings Transaction Tax (LBTT)

Generally, Land & Buildings Transaction Tax will be payable on commercial and non-commercial forests and woodlands at the lower 'Non-Residential' rates.

Tax and Transfer of Forests and Woodlands

Usually, offer documents for the purchase of forests or woodlands make it a condition that the seller confirms or guarantees that the sale of the woodland to the purchaser will comprise an exempt supply for Value Added Tax purposes; sellers should liaise with their accountant or HMRC at an early stage and, if applicable, be prepared to provide evidence that the exemption has not been waived. There are various business reasons why an owner may have decided to waive the exemption and an option to tax will convert most grants of land or property interests from an exempt supply to a taxable supply for Value Added Tax purposes. If the seller has waived the exemption, he or she should ready evidence of the election. Generally, an option to tax applies for 20 years.

Potential purchasers should also liaise with their accountants and their land agent or forestry advisor at the earliest possible stage to ensure that their project is structured in the most tax efficient manner.

It is important to consider if what is being bought is actually a business. A working forest or woodland can be a business and in certain circumstances special transfer of a business as a going- concern (TOGC) rules apply and the sale will not be treated as a taxable supply for Value Added Tax purposes, so no Value Added Tax should be charged. If the TOGC rules are being used, it is essential that all of the conditions are met and there is no procedure for an advance ruling from HM Revenue & Customs. Advice should be taken from an accountant.

If there is to be plant, machinery and equipment included in the sale, Value Added Tax may be due.

There may be capital allowances for expenditure incurred on plant, machinery and equipment available for transfer to the purchaser. Sellers will usually be required to provide a purchaser with all necessary information to enable the purchaser to prepare capital expenditure and other income tax claims and to claim any unexpended balances of allowances.

Conclusion

In conclusion, forestry owners and managers should liaise with their land agent or forestry advisor and seek specialist tax advice from their accountant at the beginning of any new forestry project. Proactive planning is required and assets and activities should be regularly reviewed.

CHAPTER SIXTEEN

THE WOODLAND CARBON CODE

Sustainably managed forests and woodlands draw carbon dioxide from the atmosphere ("carbon sink") and store the carbon in organic matter such as wood, plant materials, forest soils and leaf litter ("carbon stock"). Often, a greater proportion of carbon is stored in forest soils than the tree biomass, particularly in peat-based soils. This process of capturing and storing carbon dioxide from the atmosphere is known as "carbon sequestration". It is thought that forests and woodlands account for approximately seventy-five per cent of the annual global exchange of carbon between the land and the atmosphere and it is recognised that trees have an important part to play in achieving climate change targets.

The Woodland Carbon Code (WCC) is a UK Government standard setting out principles and requirements for woodland carbon sequestration projects that help the UK meet targets for woodland creation and the reduction of greenhouse gas emissions. The scheme is concerned with woodland creation projects – incentivising projects which may not otherwise be financially attractive – and does not apply to land that has been forested over the previous twenty-five years.

The Code is managed by Scottish Forestry and allows landowners who are creating new woodlands to measure the carbon sequestration their woodland will achieve over the lifetime of the trees ("carbon accounting") and obtain carbon units which represent carbon dioxide removed from the atmosphere by the trees as they grow. One Woodland Carbon Unit represents one tonne of carbon dioxide equivalent removed from the atmosphere in a Woodland Carbon Code verified woodland.

Carbon units (generically known as 'carbon credits') are sought after by businesses to offset their carbon footprint in greenhouse gas (GHG) reports so the 'units' have a value and they are traded globally in carbon markets. Carbon units can be used by companies to report against UK-based emissions or to use in claims of carbon neutrality or net zero emissions.

Applicants for the scheme must register their project in the UK Woodland Carbon Registry within two years of the start of planting. There are options for 'Standard' and 'Small' sized projects. A standard project can be any size while a small project is for a net planting area of five hectares or less.

All projects must be initially validated by an independent, accredited validation/verification body who will assess the project design against the Code. A Project Design Document, describing how the project meets the Code's requirements, must be submitted together with supporting evidence. Following registration, validation should be complete within three years once the trees have been planted or, alternatively, deer control/fencing is in place if the woodlands are being created by natural regeneration.

When the project has been validated, Pending Issuance Units (PIUs) are issued for the calculated carbon units and these are listed in the UK Woodland Carbon Registry. The register records the location of projects, the predicted and actual carbon sequestration and the ownership and retirement of carbon units. These units can be traded and they are retired after they have been utilised by the end user so that they can't be double-counted.

Pending Issuance Units are required because trees are a slow-growing crop and they take time to sequester carbon. A Pending Issuance Unit is effectively a preliminary Woodland Carbon Unit, based on predicted sequestration; they can be used as part of carbon planning but they can't be used to offset greenhouse gas emissions until they have been verified and converted into Woodland Carbon Units.

There is an ongoing evaluation of the project against the standards of the Code. Projects must be verified at least at year five and thereafter every ten years from initiation. This process checks that carbon sequestration has occurred and that the project is being managed sustainably. Projects must conform to the UK Forestry Standard (Chapter Five).

The validation/verification body will check that carbon statements showing the project's predicted or actual carbon sequestration are correct. Thereafter, verified Pending Issuance Units are converted into Woodland Carbon Units.

It's free to register a woodland creation project but there are costs for validation, issuing Pending Issuance Units, verification and conversion of the Pending Issuance Units into Woodland Carbon Units. The intention is that the creation of real and verifiable carbon rights will allow landowners to sell the Units to recoup the costs of creating the new woodland while generating a new income stream, creating a legacy for future generations and using carbon money to benefit habitats, communities and the environment. Woodland Carbon Code contracts tend to be for a term of between 35 and 100 years and solicitors can advise landowners on the terms and conditions with input on market variables from land agents or forestry advisors.

CHAPTER SEVENTEEN

CONCLUSION

I hope that you have enjoyed this brief book and it has explained some of the legalities to the layman, some of the practicalities and the direction of forestry in Scotland.

The Forestry and Land Management (Scotland) Act 2018 and the Forestry Strategy are to be the basis for a new era of forestry and the multitude of benefits that our forests and woodlands can deliver to the Country's populace.

I will close with a reminder of the Forestry Strategy's 50-year vision for forestry in Scotland and the forestry objectives which are to be delivered by 2029:

Scotland's Forestry Vision

'In 2070, Scotland will have more forests and woodlands, sustainably managed and better integrated with other land uses. These will provide a more resilient, adaptable resource, with greater natural capital value, that supports a strong economy, a thriving environment and healthy and flourishing communities.'

Scotland's Forestry Objectives

- increase the contribution of forests and woodlands to Scotland's sustainable and inclusive economic growth
- improve the resilience of Scotland's forests and woodlands and increase their contribution to a healthy and high-quality environment
- increase the use of Scotland's forest and woodland resources to enable more people to improve their health, well-being and life chances

MORE BOOKS BY LAW BRIEF PUBLISHING

A selection of our other titles available now:-

'A Practical Guide to Solicitor and Client Costs – 2nd Edition' by Robin Dunne
'Constructive Dismissal – Practice Pointers and Principles' by Benjimin Burgher
'A Practical Guide to Religion and Belief Discrimination Claims in the Workplace' by Kashif Ali
'A Practical Guide to the Law of Medical Treatment Decisions' by Ben Troke
'Fundamental Dishonesty and QOCS in Personal Injury Proceedings: Law and Practice' by Jake Rowley
'A Practical Guide to the Law in Relation to School Exclusions' by Charlotte Hadfield & Alice de Coverley
'A Practical Guide to Divorce for the Silver Separators' by Karin Walker
'The Right to be Forgotten – The Law and Practical Issues' by Melissa Stock
'A Practical Guide to Planning Law and Rights of Way in National Parks, the Broads and AONBs' by James Maurici QC, James Neill et al
'A Practical Guide to Election Law' by Tom Tabori
'A Practical Guide to the Law in Relation to Surrogacy' by Andrew Powell
'A Practical Guide to Claims Arising from Fatal Accidents – 2nd Edition' by James Patience
'A Practical Guide to the Ownership of Employee Inventions – From Entitlement to Compensation' by James Tumbridge & Ashley Roughton
'A Practical Guide to Asbestos Claims' by Jonathan Owen & Gareth McAloon
'A Practical Guide to Stamp Duty Land Tax in England and Northern Ireland' by Suzanne O'Hara
'A Practical Guide to the Law of Farming Partnerships' by Philip Whitcomb

'Covid-19, Homeworking and the Law – The Essential Guide to Employment and GDPR Issues' by Forbes Solicitors
'Covid-19, Force Majeure and Frustration of Contracts – The Essential Guide' by Keith Markham
'Covid-19 and Criminal Law – The Essential Guide' by Ramya Nagesh
'Covid-19 and Family Law in England and Wales – The Essential Guide' by Safda Mahmood
'A Practical Guide to the Law of Unlawful Eviction and Harassment – 2nd Edition' by Stephanie Lovegrove
'Covid-19, Residential Property, Equity Release and Enfranchisement – The Essential Guide' by Paul Sams and Louise Uphill
'Covid-19, Brexit and the Law of Commercial Leases – The Essential Guide' by Mark Shelton
'A Practical Guide to Costs in Personal Injury Claims – 2nd Edition' by Matthew Hoe
'A Practical Guide to the General Data Protection Regulation (GDPR) – 2nd Edition' by Keith Markham
'Ellis on Credit Hire – Sixth Edition' by Aidan Ellis & Tim Kevan
'A Practical Guide to Working with Litigants in Person and McKenzie Friends in Family Cases' by Stuart Barlow
'Protecting Unregistered Brands: A Practical Guide to the Law of Passing Off' by Lorna Brazell
'A Practical Guide to Secondary Liability and Joint Enterprise Post-Jogee' by Joanne Cecil & James Mehigan
'A Practical Guide to the Pre-Action RTA Claims Protocol for Personal Injury Lawyers' by Antonia Ford
'A Practical Guide to Neighbour Disputes and the Law' by Alexander Walsh
'A Practical Guide to Forfeiture of Leases' by Mark Shelton
'A Practical Guide to Coercive Control for Legal Practitioners and Victims' by Rachel Horman

'A Practical Guide to Rights Over Airspace and Subsoil' by Daniel Gatty
'Tackling Disclosure in the Criminal Courts – A Practitioner's Guide' by Narita Bahra QC & Don Ramble
'A Practical Guide to the Law of Driverless Cars – Second Edition' by Alex Glassbrook, Emma Northey & Scarlett Milligan
'A Practical Guide to TOLATA Claims' by Greg Williams
'Artificial Intelligence – The Practical Legal Issues' by John Buyers
'A Practical Guide to the Law of Prescription in Scotland' by Andrew Foyle
'A Practical Guide to the Construction and Rectification of Wills and Trust Instruments' by Edward Hewitt
'A Practical Guide to the Law of Bullying and Harassment in the Workplace' by Philip Hyland
'How to Be a Freelance Solicitor: A Practical Guide to the SRA-Regulated Freelance Solicitor Model' by Paul Bennett
'A Practical Guide to Prison Injury Claims' by Malcolm Johnson
'A Practical Guide to the Small Claims Track' by Dominic Bright
'A Practical Guide to Advising Clients at the Police Station' by Colin Stephen McKeown-Beaumont
'A Practical Guide to Antisocial Behaviour Injunctions' by Iain Wightwick
'Practical Mediation: A Guide for Mediators, Advocates, Advisers, Lawyers, and Students in Civil, Commercial, Business, Property, Workplace, and Employment Cases' by Jonathan Dingle with John Sephton
'The Mini-Pupillage Workbook' by David Boyle
'A Practical Guide to Crofting Law' by Brian Inkster
'A Practical Guide to Spousal Maintenance' by Liz Cowell
'A Practical Guide to the Law of Domain Names and Cybersquatting' by Andrew Clemson
'A Practical Guide to the Law of Gender Pay Gap Reporting' by Harini Iyengar

'A Practical Guide to the Rights of Grandparents in Children Proceedings' by Stuart Barlow
'NHS Whistleblowing and the Law' by Joseph England
'Employment Law and the Gig Economy' by Nigel Mackay & Annie Powell
'A Practical Guide to Noise Induced Hearing Loss (NIHL) Claims' by Andrew Mckie, Ian Skeate, Gareth McAloon
'An Introduction to Beauty Negligence Claims – A Practical Guide for the Personal Injury Practitioner' by Greg Almond
'Intercompany Agreements for Transfer Pricing Compliance' by Paul Sutton
'Zen and the Art of Mediation' by Martin Plowman
'A Practical Guide to the SRA Principles, Individual and Law Firm Codes of Conduct 2019 – What Every Law Firm Needs to Know' by Paul Bennett
'A Practical Guide to Adoption for Family Lawyers' by Graham Pegg
'A Practical Guide to Industrial Disease Claims' by Andrew Mckie & Ian Skeate
'A Practical Guide to Redundancy' by Philip Hyland
'A Practical Guide to Vicarious Liability' by Mariel Irvine
'A Practical Guide to Applications for Landlord's Consent and Variation of Leases' by Mark Shelton
'A Practical Guide to Relief from Sanctions Post-Mitchell and Denton' by Peter Causton
'A Practical Guide to Equity Release for Advisors' by Paul Sams
'A Practical Guide to the Law Relating to Food' by Ian Thomas
'A Practical Guide to Financial Services Claims' by Chris Hegarty
'The Law of Houses in Multiple Occupation: A Practical Guide to HMO Proceedings' by Julian Hunt
'A Practical Guide to Unlawful Eviction and Harassment' by Stephanie Lovegrove
'Occupiers, Highways and Defective Premises Claims: A Practical Guide Post-Jackson – 2nd Edition' by Andrew Mckie

www.ingramcontent.com/pod-product-compliance
Ingram Content Group UK Ltd.
Pitfield, Milton Keynes, MK11 3LW, UK
UKHW020150290926
15471UKWH00004B/789